APPLES

Rhoda Nottridge

Illustrations by John Yates

Carolrhoda Books, Inc./Minneapolis

All words that appear in **bold** are
explained in the glossary on page 30.

First published in the U.S. in 1991 by
Carolrhoda Books, Inc.

Library of Congress Cataloging-in-Publication Data

Nottridge, Rhoda.
    Apples / Rhoda Nottridge ; illustrations by John Yates.
        p.   cm. — (Foods we eat)
    Reprint. Originally published: Hove, East Sussex :
Wayland Publishers, 1990.
    Includes index.
    Summary: Surveys the history of apples from the wild crab
apple to modern-day cultivation, production, and role in
nutrition. Includes recipes for desserts and salad.
    ISBN 0-87614-655-8 (lib. bdg.)
    1. Apple — Juvenile literature. 2. Cookery (Apples) —
Juvenile literature. [1. Apple.] I. Yates, John, 1939–
ill. II. Title. III. Series: Foods we eat (Minneapolis,
Minn.)
SB363.N67   1991   90-44776
641.3′411 — dc20   CIP
                                                     AC

Printed in Italy by G. Canale C.S.p.A., Turin
Bound in the United States of America

1 2 3 4 5 6 7 8 9 10 00 99 98 97 96 95 94 93 92 91

Contents

All kinds of apples

Crab apple

Golden Delicious

Delicious

McIntosh

There are thousands of different varieties of apples in the world, and most people have their favorites. In the United States, just three varieties— Delicious (also called Red Delicious), Golden Delicious, and McIntosh—make up more than half of all apples grown and marketed. Granny Smiths are favored by Australians and Argentinians. Cox's

Orange Pippin has long been popular in England.

Apples can be divided into four groups. First there are small, sour-tasting apples called crab apples. Crab apples are not good to eat fresh, although jelly and jam can be made from some of them. There are apples used to make juice and cider and others used for baking and cooking. The best baking apples are often tart or bitter when raw but taste good when they have been cooked. The last type of apple is the dessert apple. Dessert

Rhode Island Greening

Cox's Orange Pippin

Granny Smith

Jonagold

apples vary in size, shape, and color, but all are good to eat right off the tree.

Fruit growers combine the best apples in **hybrid** varieties. The orange-colored hybrid named Jonagold is a cross between a Jonathan and a Golden Delicious apple.

Different varieties of apples from many countries are sold at markets.

Dessert apples like these Granny Smiths and Cox's Orange Pippins are specially grown for good flavor and color.

The Golden Delicious apple grew by chance from a seedling. In 1914, this sweet, yellow-colored apple was entered in a contest. It was so delicious that one of the judges tracked the tree down and bought it from the surprised West Virginia farmer for $5000. To protect his investment, the new owner had a burglar-proof steel cage fitted around the tree!

The ancient apple

All the types of apples we eat today originally came from wild apples that grew in southwestern Asia. People have been eating apples since prehistoric times. The first apples were sour. Gradually people grew better-tasting apples by taking shoots from a tree whose fruit they liked and **grafting**, or fixing, them onto other trees to grow more fruit.

Apples have been cultivated for thousands of years. This apple orchard is in full bloom.

The ancient Greeks used grafting to grow several varieties. The Romans grew apples in special tree farms, or **orchards**. They brought their favorite kinds of apples to Europe during their conquests and taught Europeans how to grow the fruit.

Much later, colonists took apples to North America. The settlers learned about many plants from Native Americans and shared their apple seeds in return. Pioneers moving west were often surprised to find orchards planted by Native Americans.

Food for the world

Apples are about 85% water, but they also contain vitamins, minerals, sugar, and **fiber** — the coarse part of apple pulp that helps in digestion. Biting into a crisp apple is also good for teeth and gums. The old saying, "Eat an apple going to bed, make the doctor beg his bread," is true today; we just say it in a different way.

Apples are one of the world's leading fruit crops. They are an important crop in Italy, Germany, France, and in the United States,

Roadside stands sell apples in late summer and fall after harvest.

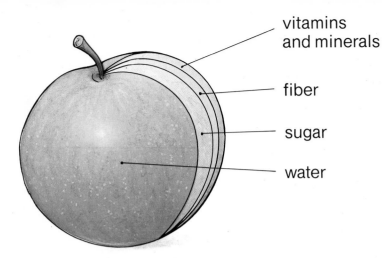

vitamins and minerals

fiber

sugar

water

Left: An apple is made up of all these substances in the different amounts shown.

Below: It is important to eat some fresh fruit every day, because fruit provides us with vitamins, minerals, and fiber.

where 9 billion pounds of apples are grown each year.

Apples are usually grown in areas with a temperate climate, where temperatures in the winter are moderate and it is warm in the summer. However, apples have been grown successfully in hot countries in the Middle East and North Africa. Some trees have even survived in the freezing cold climate of Siberia in the Soviet Union.

In the United States, Washington, Michigan, and New York states have the best climate for growing apples. Together, these three states produce over 100,000,000 bushels in an average year.

Growing apples

The pretty white or pink blossom of the apple tree in early summer has an important purpose. Its flowers attract bees, which carry pollen from one apple blossom to another. In **cross-pollination**, the pollen fertilizes eggs inside the flower. The eggs develop into seeds, and the rest of the flower grows into the fleshy tissue and outer skin of the apple.

You can grow an apple tree yourself from a seed,

but the apples that grow may not be as good as the ones that the apple seeds came from. Most growers start new trees by taking a shoot or bud and fixing it to a growing tree.

Growers start with a specially bred root called a **rootstock**, which is made by cutting off the top of a tree with good, strong roots. Rootstocks are chosen for their ability to survive cold, pests, and diseases.

Apple trees grown from seeds will not be the same as the parent trees. Only fruit growers trying to develop new varieties grow apple trees from seeds.

Grafting
1. The scion
2. The bark is slit, and the scion is slipped in.
3. The scions are bound in place on the rootstock.
4. The end of the stock is sealed with wax.

A year-old shoot, or **scion**, is cut from the type of apple tree that the fruit farmer has chosen to grow. The scion is fixed, or grafted, to the root-stock. Wax covers the cut part of the tree to seal in moisture and keep out disease.

Another way to grow a good quality tree is by **budding**. The grower puts the bud of one tree under the bark of a rootstock. The bud is bound in and will grow into the rootstock. Any other buds and branches are cut off.

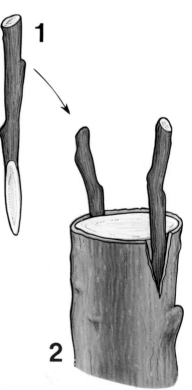

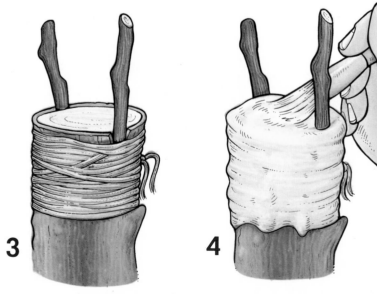

14

Right: Pruning is done in the winter when the tree is growing very slowly.

Below: In budding, the bark is slit, the bud is slipped into it, and both are firmly bound.

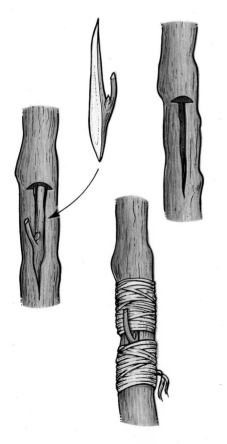

Apple trees can grow to a height of 13 to 19 feet. Nowadays, farmers often grow smaller trees, so the fruit is easier to pick. Depending on the variety, a tree needs to be 6 to 10 years old to produce good fruit.

During those years, the farmer pays close attention to **pruning** the young trees—cutting away dead wood and unnecessary branches. Trees are normally pruned in a wide-bottomed pyramid shape. Pruning helps remaining branches grow stronger and creates more light and space between branches to encourage bigger fruit and new shoots.

Apple enemies

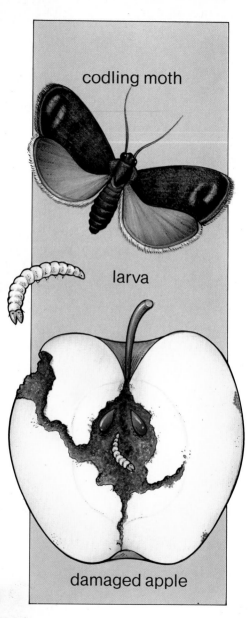

codling moth

larva

damaged apple

Humans are not alone in liking apple trees and their fruit. Many pests are also attracted to the trees. Caterpillars eat the leaves, and aphids— tiny insects—attack the branches and roots of the trees. A disease called **apple scab** is also a problem. This fungus creates cracks and black spots on infected fruit. The worst enemy of the apple tree is probably the codling moth. The female moth lays her eggs on the leaves. When the larvae, or caterpillars, hatch, they eat their way right through the apples.

Farmers usually spray trees regularly with chemicals called **pesticides** that kill insect pests living on trees. Farmers are careful not to spray when trees are in bloom, because this could kill the bees that pollinate the flowers. Pesticides can be helpful, but sometimes some of their poisons stay on the apple. That's one reason why it is important to wash fruit carefully before you eat it.

Some farmers use insects to fight back against pests. The ladybird beetle, for example, has an appetite for red mites, insects that feed on apple trees.

Fruit growers are constantly trying to create new breeds of apples that are more resistant to disease and less attractive to insects.

Above: Black scab is one of the most common apple diseases. It is a fungus that attacks the surface of the apple.

Left: Farmers spray their crops with pesticides to destroy harmful insects and diseases and to keep the apples healthy.

From farm to store

Above: Dessert apples are picked by hand, because machines might bruise the fruit.

Right: Special small, or dwarf, trees make picking the apples easier.

Most varieties of apples are ready for harvesting in late summer or autumn. The fruit is ready to be picked when the apple stalk comes away easily from the tree. Dessert apples are picked by hand from the ground or on ladders. When the pickers' sacks or buckets are full, they empty them into large bins. Apples used for cider, juice, vinegar, apple butter, apple jellies, and applesauce are

The apples are sorted by size and quality before they are packed.

often picked by machines.

A tractor with hydraulic arms gently scoops up the bins of apples and carries them to the storage plant. Here, the bins of apples are sometimes sprayed with chemicals to stop any rot from spreading. The apples are then kept in a cool place to await packing.

At some packing houses, the apples are lowered into a tank of water. This washes the fruit and gets rid of any leaves. The apples then bob along onto a conveyor belt, where they are dried. The belts are covered with rubber to avoid bruising the apples.

Next comes **grading**, where apples are sorted into groups by size. They either fall into gaps in the conveyor belt according to their size or pass over a machine that weighs and sorts them.

The packers at the end of the conveyor belt check apples carefully to make sure they are not damaged or diseased. The smallest apples may be used for cider. Medium-sized eating and baking apples may be packaged in plastic bags to be sold

After the apples have been picked, they may be washed to remove leaves, twigs, and pests.

Some apples are wrapped so that they do not touch each other. This stops bruising and keeps rot from spreading.

in stores. The best dessert apples are packed in boxes, either on trays or wrapped in paper to prevent damage.

Some apples are sorted quickly and shipped directly to stores, while others stay in cold storage for many months. While in storage, apples take in oxygen and give off carbon dioxide in a way that resembles breathing. In **controlled atmosphere storage**, apples are stored in sealed rooms where the amount of oxygen in the air is lowered. With less oxygen in the air, apples "breathe" more slowly and stay fresh longer.

Making cider

Cider has been made since ancient times. It was especially important in Colonial America, since new settlers thought the water was unsafe for drinking. Instead they drank cider, a mildly alcoholic drink made from apples.

First they crushed apples in a cider mill. The apple juice that came out was set aside. The

Cider and apple juice are made from crushed apples.

crushed apple, called **pomace**, was placed in a vat and mixed with air. The pomace was then formed into thick slabs, or "cheeses," which were stacked and pressed. The juice that came out was kept for cider, and the crushed apples were fed to the pigs.

Yeast feeds on the sugar in the apple juice and turns it into alcohol and gas. This bubbly process, called **fermentation**, is the final step in turning juice into alcoholic cider.

Today, cider is made in factories. What we call apple cider is really apple juice. **Hard cider** like the colonists made is still a popular drink in many parts of the world.

The juice for making cider is squeezed out of the apples by a heavy weight. Modern cider mills use mechanical cider presses.

The famous apple

The humble apple appears in many stories, sayings, and legends from around the world. Many people have heard the story of Johnny Appleseed, for example, but most don't know that he was a real man named John Chapman.

John was born in Leominster, Massachusetts, in 1774, but he didn't stay there long. For almost 50 years, he planted apple seeds in the Midwest when it was still a rough frontier.

Although stories about Chapman can't be proven, people said that he lived in the open, wore a cloth sack for a shirt and rags for shoes, and used a cooking pot for a hat. (The pot was also used for cooking.) He generously gave apple seeds to the new settlers and often gave a short sermon as well, since he was a very religious man.

Soon, people began calling him Johnny

Appleseed and telling stories about his kindness. A gentle man, Johnny grew apple trees only from seeds and never pruned, because grafting and pruning would hurt the plants.

Bobbing for apples is a good party game. Keep your arms behind your back and pick up an apple with your teeth.

Baked apples

You will need, for five baked apples:

5 cooking apples
1/3 cup chopped walnuts
1/3 cup raisins
water

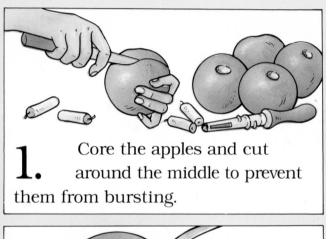

1. Core the apples and cut around the middle to prevent them from bursting.

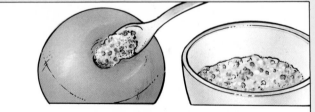

2. Mix the walnuts and raisins in a bowl and stuff the empty cores with the mixture.

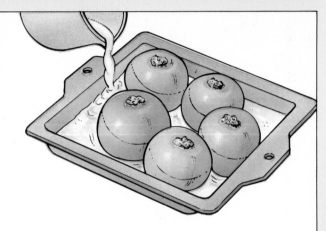

3. Put in a greased baking dish and add water to the bottom of the dish to a depth of 1/2 inch.

4. Bake in a 350°F oven for 50 minutes. Sweeten the baked apples with honey if you like.

Waldorf salad

You will need:

3 large red dessert apples
2 tablespoons lemon juice
3 sticks celery
4 tablespoons mayonnaise
4 tablespoons plain yogurt
½ cup chopped walnuts

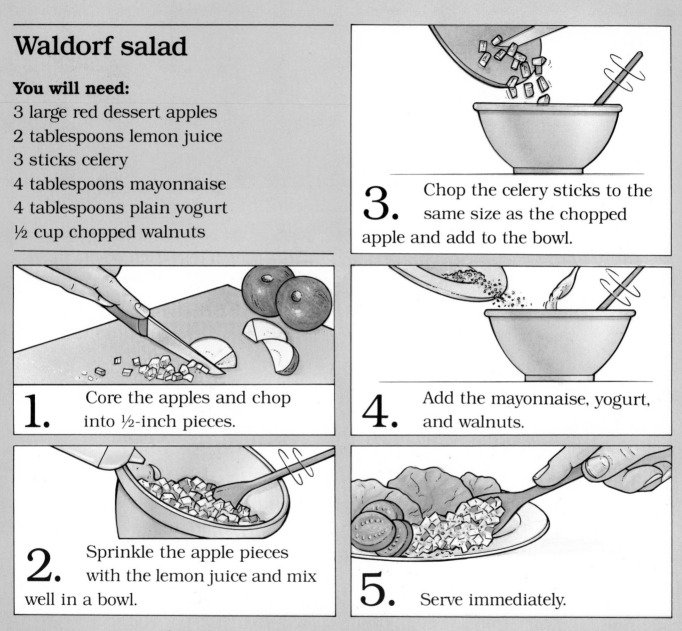

1. Core the apples and chop into ½-inch pieces.

2. Sprinkle the apple pieces with the lemon juice and mix well in a bowl.

3. Chop the celery sticks to the same size as the chopped apple and add to the bowl.

4. Add the mayonnaise, yogurt, and walnuts.

5. Serve immediately.

Apple muffins

You will need, for 10 muffins:

2 tablespoons butter or margarine
3 dessert apples
1 teaspoon cinnamon
2 tablespoons sugar
1 cup all-purpose flour
1 teaspoon salt
1½ teaspoons baking powder
2 tablespoons sugar
1 egg
1 teaspoon milk

2. Peel and core two apples and cut across each one to make five thick apple rings. Peel, core, and chop the remaining apple.

1. Melt butter in a pan and set aside. Lightly grease a muffin tin and preheat oven to 425°F.

3. Mix the cinnamon and sugar in a bowl and dip the apple rings into the mixture until they are coated.

4. Sift the flour, salt, baking powder, and sugar. Beat the egg, milk, and melted butter together. Quickly stir in the flour mixture.

5. Fold in the chopped apple and fill the muffin tins one-third full with batter. Top each with an apple ring. Bake for 20-25 minutes at 425°F. Serve hot with butter.

Glossary

apple scab: a fungus that attacks apple trees, leaving cracks and black spots on fruit

budding: the process of growing a particular variety of apple by placing a bud under the bark of a rootstock

controlled atmosphere storage: airtight storage areas where air flow is controlled to keep apples fresh

cross-pollination: the process that occurs when bees carry the pollen from one blossom to another, fertilizing the flower

fermentation: the bubbly chemical reaction that takes place when yeasts in unpasteurized apple juice mix with air and sugars, producing alcohol and gas

fiber: the coarse, pulpy part of the apple

grading: the process of sorting apples by size, weight, or color before packaging and shipping

grafting: a way of growing a particular variety of apple by attaching a year-old shoot to a rootstock

hard cider: a mildly alcoholic drink made from fermented apple juice

hybrid: the offspring of two plants of different varieties

orchards: fruit tree farms where many trees are grown together in widely spaced rows

pesticides: chemicals that kill insects and other pests

pomace: the crushed apple that is left over when juice is pressed out of apples during cider making

pruning: the process of cutting off dead wood and unnecessary branches from a growing tree

rootstock: the root and tree trunk used in grafting and budding. Rootstocks are bred for strong roots, resistance to disease and pests, and ability to withstand extreme temperatures.

scion: a year-old shoot or branch that is grafted onto a rootstock. The scion determines what kind of fruit the tree will bear.

Index

Photo acknowledgments

The photographs in this book were provided by: pp. 6, 7, 9 (right), 17 (left), 18 (bottom), 21, ZEFA; pp. 8 (Leonard Lee Rue), 10 (Leonard Lee Rue), 17 (top, Eric Crichton), Bruce Coleman; pp. 9 (top), 18 (top), Topham Picture Library; pp. 11 (right), 23, Hutchison Library; pp. 15 (top), 19, 20, 22, Wayland Picture Library; p. 25, Paul Seheult. Cover photograph by Peter Stiles.

641.3   Nottridge, Rhoda
Not
        Apples

DATE DUE